Growing Things

Green and Growing

A Book About Plants

Written by Susan Blackaby

Illustrated by Charlene DeLage

Content Adviser: Jeffrey H. Gillman, Ph.D., Assistant Professor
Horticultural Science, University of Minnesota, St. Paul, Minnesota

Reading Adviser: Susan Kesselring, M.A., Literacy Educator
Rosemount-Apple Valley-Eagan (Minnesota) School District

PICTURE WINDOW BOOKS
Minneapolis, Minnesota

Editor: Nadia Higgins
Designer: Nathan Gassman
Page production: Picture Window Books
The illustrations in this book were painted with watercolor.

Picture Window Books
5115 Excelsior Boulevard
Suite 232
Minneapolis, MN 55416
1-877-845-8392
www.picturewindowbooks.com

Printed in the United States of America.
1 2 3 4 5 6 08 07 06 05 04 03

Library of Congress Cataloging-in-Publication Data
Blackaby, Susan.
Green and growing : a book about plants / written by Susan Blackaby ; illustrated by Charlene DeLage.
v. cm. — (Growing things)
Contents: All kind of plants—How plants are alike—How plants are different—
How you use plants—Through the garden gate—Fun facts—The life cycle of a plant.
ISBN 1-4048-0107-3 (lib. bdg.)
1. Plants—Juvenile literature. 2. Plants. I. DeLage, Charlene, 1944– ill. II. Title.
QK49 .B526 2003
581—dc21
2002156340

Table of Contents

All Kinds of Plants

How is a maple tree like a daffodil?

How is a blade of grass like a rosebush?

4

All of these are living things.

All of these are living things called plants.

A plant can be a tree or a shrub.

A plant can be a flower or a trailing vine.

No matter what they look like or where they live,
all green, growing things are alike in some ways.

How Plants Are Alike

Green plants make their own food to grow healthy and strong.

They use their roots to soak up water.

They use their green parts to soak up air and sunlight.
They use the air, water, and sunlight to make the food they need.

Plants cannot move from place to place the way animals do.

Their roots keep them rooted to one spot.

Animals, wind, and water carry plant seeds to new places where they can grow.

Plants do not have senses, but they react to light.

They grow up toward the sunlight.

They grow around things that get in their way.

Daisy Means Day's Eye
The daisy's flower opens in the morning. The flower head turns as it follows the sun across the sky. It closes at sunset.

11

How Plants Are Different

Many plants, like poppies and peach trees, have roots, stems, and leaves. They have flowers and seeds, too. The seeds can be inside of pods or fruit.

Some plants, like firs and pines and cedars, have needles instead of leaves.

They have seed cones instead of fruit.

Some plants, like grasses, do not have real stems.

Plants can come in all sizes, shapes, and colors.

The smallest plant on Earth is duckweed.

Duckweed is not much bigger than the period at the end of this sentence.

The biggest plant on Earth is the giant redwood.

A very old redwood can be as tall as a 20-story skyscraper.

Plants can grow every which way. Some plants creep along the ground. Some plants grow tall and straight. Some plants climb walls or cliffs.

20154002

Plants can grow almost anywhere.

Cactus plants find and store water in the hot, dry desert.

Pine trees grow tall on windy, snowy mountain slopes.

Cattails and reeds like boggy, soggy ground.
Lily of the valley grows best in cool, dark places.

How You Use Plants

Think about how you use plants every day. Plants give off oxygen when they make their food. You breathe the oxygen in the air.

You eat plant parts.

Your body uses the energy that was stored in the plants.

What Plant Parts Do You Eat?

Roots: Carrots, Radishes

Stems: Rhubarb, Potato

Leaves: Lettuce, Spinach

Fruits: Bananas, Oranges, Tomatoes, Cucumbers

Seeds: Rice, Corn, Peanuts

Flowers: Brussels Sprouts, Broccoli, Cauliflower

It takes lots of plants to make one bag lunch.

Your shirt, pants, socks, and sneakers came from a cotton plant.

The tree used to make the table grew from a seed no bigger than your thumb.

Parts of a tree were even used to make the bag!

People depend on a world of sprouting seeds, blooming bushes, and towering trees. Think of all the amazing plants that grow in our garden called Earth!

Through the Garden Gate

Draw a picture of a garden.
How many plants are growing there?
Add these things to your garden:

- trees with fruit
- trees with cones
- shrubs and bushes
- flowers
- fruits and vegetables
- climbers and vines

Fun Facts

- The oldest tree on Earth is more than 5,000 years old.

- Cork for bottle stoppers and for bulletin boards comes from the bark of the cork oak tree.

- Rubber comes from a plant that grows in South America and other warm places.

- Maple syrup comes from the sap of sugar maple trees. At the end of winter, the sap flows up the trunk from the roots to give the tree energy.

- Bamboo is tall and woody like a tree, but it is really the tallest grass in the world.

- Mosses, algae, and ferns were the first plants that grew on Earth. Outlines of these plants can be found in rocks that are millions of years old.

Life Cycle of a Plant

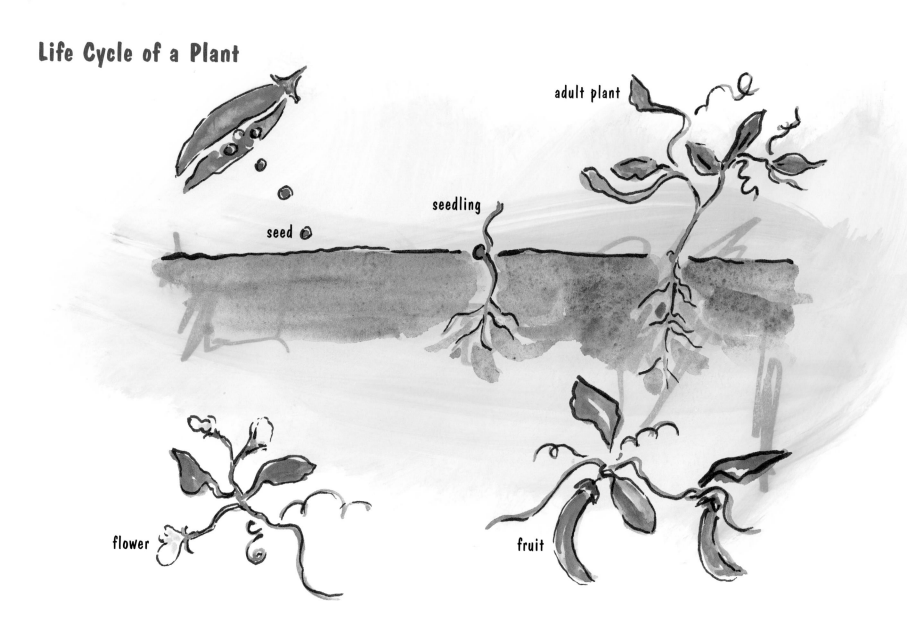

seed

seedling

adult plant

flower

fruit

Words to Know

cone—a scaly fruit that holds seeds

fruit—a part of a plant that holds seeds

root—the part of a plant that soaks up water and nutrients. Most roots are under the ground.

seed—a part of a plant that holds everything needed to make a new plant

stem—the part of a plant that connects the roots to the leaves

To Learn More

At the Library

Hammersmith, Craig. *Watch It Grow.* Minneapolis: Compass Point Books, 2002.

Royston, Angela. *How Plants Grow.* Des Plaines, Ill.: Heinemann Library, 1999.

Spilsbury, Louise. *Plant Growth.* Chicago: Heinemann Library, 2002.

On the Web

EPA Kids' Site
http://www.epa.gov/kids
For information about exploring and protecting nature

Native Plant Guide
http://www.enature.com/guides/select_LBJNative.asp
For photos of and information on over 1,000 kinds of plants

Want more information about plants? FACT HOUND offers a safe, fun way to find Web sites. All of the sites on Fact Hound have been researched by our staff. Simply follow these steps:

1. Visit *http://www.facthound.com.*
2. Enter a search word or 1404801073.
3. Click Fetch It.

Your trusty Fact Hound will fetch the best sites for you!

Index

24